101 Things®
To Do With
Meatballs

D1304857

101 Things® To Do With Meatballs

BY
STEPHANIE
ASHCRAFT

10/10

GIBBS SMITH
TO ENRICH AND INSPIRE HUMANKIND

Salt Lake City | Charleston | Santa Fe | Santa Barbara

First Edition
13 12 11 10 09   20 19 18 17 16 15 14 13 12 11 10 9 8 7 6 5 4 3 2

Text © 2009 Stephanie Ashcraft
Casa Di Bertacchi® and Farm Rich® are registered trademarks of
Rich Products Corporation.

Published by
Gibbs Smith
P.O. Box 667
Layton, Utah 84041

Orders: 1.800.835.4993
www.gibbs-smith.com

Printed and bound in Korea
Gibbs Smith books are printed on either recycled, 100%
post consumer waste, or FSC certified papers.

Library of Congress Cataloging-in-Publication Data

Ashcraft, Stephanie.
  101 things to do with meatballs / Stephanie Ashcraft. — 1st ed.
     p. cm.
  ISBN-13: 978-1-4236-0588-1
  ISBN-10: 1-4236-0588-8
  1. Meatballs. I. Title. II. Title: One hundred one things to do with
meatballs. III. Title: One hundred and one things to do with meatballs.
  TX749.A84 2009
  641.8'24—dc22

                         2008034294

A heart felt thanks to Byron Shefchik, Kathy Ask, Kevin Bankston, Susan Axel Bedsaul, Barrie Carmel, Scott Corey, Deanna Day, Barbara Dieterman, Kathy Emerson, Lisa Giberson, Lorien Godsey, Tamie Griffith, Jenna Guthrie, Jayne Mathews, Jamie McKeon, Tony Nardello, Louis Pugliese, Linda F. Sallins, and Anna K. Wilson of Casa Di Bertacchi® and Farm Rich® for providing ideas and all the ingredients to make this book possible. Thank you, Byron and team, for the faith, encouragement, and support that you have given me.

Thanks also to all my neighbors, friends, and family who helped with taste testing and with my children while I worked on this book. I especially would not have survived without the extra help at home from Robin Morse, the Kimbers, and the Deggingers. I love you all.

CONTENTS

• *Italian-Style Cocktail Meatballs 58* • *Blue Cheese Buffalo Balls 59* • *Sports Day Meatballs 60* • *Magnificent Meatballs 61* • *Saucy Meatballs 62* • *Teriyaki Meatballs 63* • *Maple Meatballs 64* • *Feta Meatballs with Cucumber Yogurt Sauce 65* • *Spicy Jamaican Jerk Meatballs 66* • *Asian Meatball Appetizers 67* • *Ginger Ale Meatballs 68* • *Cheesy Meatballs 69* • *Salsa Verde Meatballs 70* • *Holiday Meatballs 71* • *Sour Cream–Sauced Meatballs 72*

Pasta Dinners

Meatball Fettuccine Alfredo 74 • *Chipotle Meatball Pasta 75* • *Florentine Meatballs and Noodles 76* • *Meatballs in Blue Cheese Sauce 77* • *Slow-Cooked Tomato Soup Meatballs 78* • *Easy Meatball Lasagna 79* • *Pesto Spaghetti and Meatballs 80* • *Ricotta-Stuffed Shells and Meatballs 81* • *Baked Ziti and Meatballs 82* • *Eggplant Parmesan 83* • *Italian-Tossed Tortellini 84* • *Ravioli Meatball Stir-Fry 85* • *Meatball Stroganoff 86* • *Amazing Meatball Tortellini 87* • *Cheesy Broccoli Meatballs 88*

Dinners with Rice

Easy Rice and Meatballs 90 • *Meatballs in Curry Sauce 91* • *Sesame Stir-Fry 92* • *Swiss Mushroom Meatball Casserole 93* • *Creamy Meatball and Brown Rice Casserole 94* • *Pineapple Meatballs and Rice 95* • *Meatballs with Orange Peanut Sauce 96* • *Cajun Shrimp and Meatball Goulash 97* • *Creamy French Onion Meatballs 98* • *Meatballs with Apricot Hoisin Sauce 99* • *Enchilada Meatballs 100* • *Creamy Rice and Meatballs 101* • *Taste of the Islands Meatballs 102*

Family Favorites

Meatballs in Tomato and Corn Sauce 104 • *Sweet and Sour Meatball Kabobs 105* • *Caesar Meatball Kabobs 106* • *Breakfast Burritos 107* • *Easy Meatball Pizza 108* • *Southwest Crescent Pockets 109* • *Meatball Pot Pie 110* • *Instant Soft Taco 111* • *Meatball Fajita Quesadillas 112* • *Baked Beefy Mac and Cheese 113* • *Stuffing-Covered Meatball Casserole 114* • *Enchilada Casserole 115* • *Spicy Meatball Burritos 116* • *Tater Tot Kid's Casserole 117* • *Hash Brown Meatball Casserole 118* • *Kid-Friendly Taco Casserole 119*

HELPFUL HINTS

Welcome to the wonderful world of meatballs! Now, more than ever, families are faced with a common problem: our hectic lives leave very little time for preparing nutritious, well-balanced meals. As a mom of four, I had the challenge of fitting my love for cooking and my desire to feed my family nutritiously into my busy schedule. I applied my knowledge and experience with food preparation and eventually developed the "101" cookbook concept.

This book provides you with 101 delicious recipes, all made with a comfort food favorite—meatballs! I hope you'll find that with so many simple, delicious, and nutritious recipes, everyone's appetite will be appeased.

Meatballs are such a versatile food and so easy to prepare. As a mom, I put love into every meal I make. That means I make sure to serve high-quality meatballs to my family and guests. I don't have time to make meatballs from scratch, so I buy frozen, fully cooked meatballs in a big bag from the store. There are lots of brands that you can choose from. Unfortunately, some of them are not so tasty. To help with your shopping, I've listed several hints to let you know which brands have worked the best for me, as well as my tips on thawing and cooking.

1. Choose a brand you recognize. For some large manufacturers, meatballs are simply a by-product of their other meat businesses. Make sure to pick a brand that specializes in meatballs, such as Casa Di Bertacchi® and Farm Rich,® to ensure you always have a high-quality selection.

2. Choose the flavor you crave. The most common flavors of meatballs are original (also known as home-style), Italian-style, and Swedish. My favorite is the Casa Di Bertacchi® Italian-style meatballs as well as Farm Rich® Original and Italian-Style meatballs. Their seasonings don't overpower the other flavors in the recipes. Plus, both of those brands make meatballs the same way Italians have been making them for generations—seared, and then steamed until fully cooked.

3. Choose the right size meatball. I used Casa Di Bertacchi® ⅝-ounce meatballs in every recipe. Farm Rich® also makes a great ½-ounce size. A conversion chart has been included for your convenience. Most recipes in this book are better suited for an appetizer-size meatball, such as ½ ounce (as Farm Rich® makes) or ⅝ ounce (as Casa Di Bertacchi® makes).

Meatball Conversion Chart—Number of Meatballs by Weight												
	Net Weight											
Meatball Size	4 oz	8 oz	10 oz	12 oz	16 oz	24 oz	32 oz	38 oz	40 oz	4 lb	5 lb	6 lb
½ in	8	16	20	24	32	48	64	76	80	128	160	192
⅝ in	6	13	16	19	26	38	51	61	64	102	128	154
1 in	4	8	10	12	16	24	32	38	40	64	80	96
1.5 in	3	5	7	8	11	16	21	25	27	43	53	64
2 in	2	4	5	6	8	12	16	19	20	32	40	48

4. Choose your desired blend of meat. Many people prefer to buy meatballs made with 100 percent beef, such as those made by Casa Di Bertacchi.® However, a beef and pork blend (like Farm Rich® meatballs) tastes nearly identical and can be less costly. Turkey is another option that will also work in these recipes.

5. Choose a good-size bag. Because meatballs are such a versatile food, I recommend keeping a big bag of them in your freezer at all times. Casa Di Bertacchi® currently sells 6-pound bags in club stores and Farm Rich® offers a 2-pound bag.

6. Thaw meatballs properly. Frozen meatballs should be thawed in the refrigerator, or they can be thawed using the defrost function on a microwave.

7. Cook the meatballs properly. While frozen meatballs are already fully cooked, they should be reheated to at least 160 degrees to ensure they are safe for eating. Heating meatballs can be done by baking, microwaving, heating in a sauce, or even grilling. My favorite way to reheat a meatball is by steaming. To steam a meatball, simply add ½ inch of water to a baking dish and cook at 375 degrees until the meatballs reach 160 degrees. This takes around 40 minutes for several pounds of meatballs. For smaller portions, the microwave works great. Just add ½ inch of water to a microwaveable container. It takes less than 2 minutes to fully heat 5 meatballs.

APPETIZERS & SIDES

MINI MEATBALL HAMBURGERS

26 (1 pound)	**frozen, fully cooked meatballs**
1 cup	**ketchup**
3 tablespoons	**Dijon honey mustard**
26 (2-inch)	**dinner rolls,** sliced in half horizontally
1 1/2 cups	**sweet pickle relish**

Preheat oven to 400 degrees.

Place the meatballs in a 9 x 9-inch pan with 1/2 inch water. Bake for 30 minutes, or until thoroughly heated.

In a small bowl, combine ketchup and mustard. Place a heaping teaspoon of the mixture on the bottom of a roll and then top with a meatball. Add a teaspoon of pickle relish and cover with top half of roll. Repeat with remaining ingredients and serve immediately on a large platter. Makes 26 appetizers.

VARIATION: Place a small slice of cheddar cheese over each meatball to make cheeseburgers.

MEATBALL
JALAPEÑO POPPERS

13	**jalapeños,** stemmed
1 package (8 ounces)	**cream cheese,** softened
13	**frozen, fully cooked meatballs,** thawed
13 slices (1 pound)	**sliced bacon,** cut in half

Preheat oven to 375 degrees.

Slice each pepper in half lengthwise, remove the seeds, and rinse out. Spread cream cheese in each jalapeño half. Cut the meatballs in half. Place each meatball half, cut side down, over cream cheese. Wrap a half slice of bacon around each stuffed jalapeño and secure with a toothpick. Place on a baking sheet and bake 25–30 minutes, or until bacon is browned. Serve immediately on a platter. Makes 26 appetizers.

IMPORTANT NOTE: Use plastic gloves when cutting and preparing peppers to prevent skin irritation.

MEATBALL SLIDERS

1/2	**medium onion,** finely chopped
2 tablespoons	**olive oil**
2 teaspoons	**minced garlic**
1 can (28 ounces)	**crushed tomatoes**
1/2 teaspoon	**sugar**
2 teaspoons	**Italian seasoning**
3/4 teaspoon	**salt**
20	**frozen, fully cooked meatballs,** thawed
20 (2-inch)	**soft buns or rolls,** split

In a 4-quart pan, saute onion in oil until tender. Add garlic and saute 1 minute more. Stir in tomatoes, sugar, and seasoning. Simmer 10–15 minutes over medium heat, stirring occasionally. Add meatballs to the sauce. Cover pan and continue to cook over medium heat 10–15 minutes more, stirring occasionally, until meatballs are heated through. Place a meatball and 1 tablespoon sauce in the middle of each split roll. Secure each meatball to the bun with a toothpick. Serve immediately. Makes 20 appetizers.

NOTE: Any leftover sauce can be used for dipping bread sticks or serving over hot cooked pasta later.

MEATBALL BRUSCHETTA

9	**frozen, fully cooked meatballs,** thawed
1 loaf	**French baguette or crusty Italian bread**
2 tablespoons	**olive oil**
1 jar (13.75 ounces)	**bruschetta topping**
1/3 pound	**fresh full-fat mozzarella,** thinly sliced

Cut meatballs in half and heat according to package directions. Cut bread into 18 slices. Lay slices evenly over a baking sheet and brush with oil. Broil 1–2 minutes, or until lightly toasted. Place a tablespoon of the bruschetta topping over each bread slice. Top with a meatball half, cut side down. Place cheese slices over the meatballs and broil 1–2 minutes, or until the cheese melts and lightly browns. Makes 18 appetizers.

VARIATION: Use goat cheese instead of mozzarella.

BACON-WRAPPED MEATBALLS

8 slices	**uncooked bacon,** cut in half
16	**frozen, fully cooked meatballs,** thawed
	honey mustard
	barbecue sauce
	ranch dressing

Preheat oven to 375 degrees.

Wrap a half slice bacon around each meatball and secure with a toothpick. Place on a baking sheet and bake 20–25 minutes, or until bacon is crisp. Serve with honey mustard, barbecue sauce, and ranch dressing for dipping. Makes 16 appetizers.

Note: You can make as many or as few of these appetizers as you want. Simply use double the amount of meatballs than whole slices of bacon.

THAI PIZZA

I teaspoon	**dried ginger**
2 tablespoons	**olive oil**
I tube (13.8 ounces)	**refrigerated pizza crust dough**
3 tablespoons	**soy sauce**
3 tablespoons	**peanut butter**
	juice from I lime
I teaspoon	**Thai green curry paste**
13	**frozen, fully cooked meatballs,** thawed and sliced into thirds
$^{1}/_{2}$ cup	**shredded carrots**
I can (8 ounces)	**pineapple tidbits,** drained
I tablespoon	**chopped cilantro leaves**
I tablespoon	**sliced green onion**

Preheat oven to 425 degrees.

In a small bowl, combine ginger and oil; let sit 10 minutes. Spread dough on a baking sheet prepared with nonstick cooking spray. Brush olive oil mixture over dough and then bake for 5 minutes.

In a 2-quart bowl, whisk together the soy sauce, peanut butter, lime juice, and curry paste until fairly smooth. Spread mixture evenly over pizza crust. Top with remaining ingredients and bake 8–10 minutes more, or until crust is golden. Slice into six rows of four pieces. Makes 24 appetizers.

PUFF PASTRY MEATBALL AND MUSHROOM POCKETS

26 (1 pound)	**frozen, fully cooked meatballs,** thawed
2 cups	**sliced mushrooms**
1/2 cup	**chopped sweet onion**
1 teaspoon	**minced garlic**
1 tablespoon	**olive oil**
	salt and pepper
1 box (17.3 ounces)	**frozen puff pastry dough,** thawed
1	**large egg,** beaten

Preheat oven to 400 degrees.

Cut meatballs in half. In a frying pan, saute meatball halves, mushrooms, onion, and garlic in oil for 10 minutes over medium heat; salt and pepper to taste. On a cutting board, cut each sheet of puff pastry into 9 (3-inch) squares. Place a heaping tablespoon of mushroom meatball filling in the center of each square. Pull corners up to the top center and overlap over the filling. With a pastry brush, brush the tops with the egg and press to seal the pockets. Place pockets on two baking sheets and bake 16–18 minutes, or until golden brown. Makes 18 appetizers.

MALAYSIAN MEATBALLS

52 (2 pounds)	**frozen, fully cooked meatballs**
$^1/_4$ cup	**100-percent natural peanut butter** (no added sugar or oil)
$^1/_2$ cup	**warm water**
$^1/_2$ cup	**hoisin sauce**
$2^1/_2$ tablespoons	**sweet red chile sauce**

Cook meatballs according to package directions. Meanwhile, stir peanut butter until smooth. In a bowl, combine peanut butter, water, and hoisin sauce until smooth. Stir in the chile sauce. Serve meatballs with toothpicks as an appetizer with the sauce on the side for dipping. Makes 10–12 servings.

NOTE: Hoisin sauce and sweet red chile sauce can be found in the Asian section of the grocery store.

CRESCENT-WRAPPED MEATBALLS

24	**frozen, fully cooked meatballs,** thawed
2 tubes (8 ounces each)	**refrigerated crescent roll dough**
1 1/4 cups	**grated Italian-blend cheese or mozzarella and provolone marinara sauce**

Preheat oven to 400 degrees.

Cut meatballs in half. Unroll the crescent dough. Cut each crescent into 3 equal-size parts. Place a pinch of cheese over dough. Place meatball half over cheese. Wrap dough around the meatball, pinching and positioning to completely cover. Lay wrapped meatballs on a large baking sheet and bake 10–12 minutes, or until dough is golden brown. Serve with marinara sauce for dipping. Makes 48 appetizers.

SOUTHWEST TACO SALAD

13	**frozen, fully cooked meatballs,** thawed
2 tablespoons	**taco seasoning**
1/3 cup	**water**
1	**large head romaine lettuce,** torn into bite-size pieces
1 cup	**cooked red kidney beans**
1 cup	**grape tomatoes**
1 cup	**grated sharp cheddar cheese**
2 cups	**crushed Doritos,** any flavor
1 bottle (16 ounces)	**Catalina dressing**

Cut meatballs in half. In a frying pan, combine meatball halves, taco seasoning, and water. Simmer over medium heat for 8 minutes.

In a large bowl, layer lettuce, meatballs, beans, tomatoes, cheese, and chips. Serve with Catalina dressing on the side. Makes 6–8 servings.

PARMESAN MEATBALL BISCUITS

1 tube (12 ounces)	**refrigerated layer biscuits**
10	**frozen, fully cooked meatballs,** thawed
2 tablespoons	**grated Parmesan cheese**
1/2 teaspoon	**dried Italian seasoning**
1/4 teaspoon	**garlic powder**
	marinara sauce

Preheat oven to 375 degrees.

Separate dough into 10 biscuits and flatten slightly. Place a meatball in the center of each biscuit and wrap dough completely around it, sealing the edges. Place the sealed side down in an 8-inch round pan. Evenly space the biscuits in the pan.

In a small bowl, combine the cheese, Italian seasoning, and garlic powder. Press a pinch of the cheese mixture into the top of each roll. Bake for 15–20 minutes, or until golden brown. Serve with warm marinara sauce for dipping. Makes 10 servings.

EASY MEATBALL NACHOS

16	**frozen, fully cooked meatballs,** thawed
1	**medium onion,** chopped
1	**green bell pepper,** seeded and chopped
1 tablespoon	**olive oil**
1 envelope	**taco seasoning**
1 can (14.5 ounces)	**sliced stewed tomatoes,** with liquid
1 can (15 ounces)	**black beans,** rinsed and drained
1 bag (10 ounces or larger)	**tortilla chips,** any variety
	grated cheddar or Monterey Jack cheese
	sour cream, optional

Cut meatballs into quarters. In a large frying pan, saute the onion and bell pepper in oil over medium-high heat until tender. Stir in meatballs and cook for 3 minutes. Stir in taco seasoning, tomatoes, and beans. Reduce heat to medium and simmer 10 minutes, stirring occasionally and breaking apart tomato chunks. Spoon mixture over individual servings of tortilla chips. Sprinkle cheese over top and garnish with sour cream if desired. Makes 8–10 servings.

VARIATION: Filling can also be served burrito style in warm soft flour tortillas.

SOUP, STEWS, & CHILI

MEATBALL MINESTRONE

2 cans (15 ounces each)	**cannellini or Great Northern beans,** rinsed and drained, divided
1 box (32 ounces)	**chicken broth**
2 cups	**water**
1 tablespoon	**minced garlic**
1 envelope	**dry vegetable soup or dip mix**
26 (1 pound)	**frozen, fully cooked meatballs,** thawed
1 can (14.5 ounces)	**diced tomatoes with basil, garlic, and oregano,** with liquid
8 ounces	**uncooked rainbow rotini pasta**
1 bag (9 ounces)	**fresh spinach,** torn
	grated Parmesan cheese, optional

In a 5- to 6-quart stockpot, combine 1 can beans, broth, water, and garlic over medium-high heat and bring to a boil. Add dry vegetable mix, stirring thoroughly. Stir in meatballs and tomatoes and return to a boil; stir in pasta. Cover and simmer over medium heat for 15 minutes, stirring occasionally. Add remaining can of beans and spinach; simmer 5 minutes more. Garnish with cheese if desired. Makes 12–15 servings.

TORTELLINI MEATBALL STEW

1 container (32 ounces)	**beef broth**
4 cups	**water**
26 (1 pound)	**frozen, fully cooked meatballs**
1 cup	**chunky salsa**
1 teaspoon	**minced garlic**
1/2 tablespoon	**Italian seasoning**
1 bag (16 ounces)	**frozen Italian-style vegetable mix**
1 bag (19 ounces)	**frozen cheese tortellini**
	salt and pepper

In a 5- to 6-quart stockpot, combine broth, water, meatballs, salsa, garlic, and Italian seasoning; bring to a boil. Simmer over medium-high heat for 10 minutes. Add vegetables and return to a boil. Simmer over medium-high heat for 6 minutes. Stir in tortellini and bring to a boil. Boil for 5 minutes. Salt and pepper to taste. Makes 8–10 servings.

FAMILY FAVORITE EGG NOODLE SOUP

I bag (16 ounces)	**frozen egg noodles**
I	**medium onion,** diced
2 stalks	**celery,** sliced into small pieces
2 tablespoons	**olive oil**
26 (I pound)	**frozen, fully cooked meatballs**
I box (32 ounces)	**beef broth**
2 cups	**water**
2 teaspoons	**dried parsley flakes** (or 2 table-spoons fresh chopped parsley)
I teaspoon	**salt**
I teaspoon	**ground black pepper**

Thaw noodles according to package directions. In a 4-quart soup pan, saute the onion and celery in oil over high heat for 3 minutes, stirring occasionally. Add meatballs to the pan. Saute for 3 minutes more, stirring occasionally. Mix in broth, water, parsley, salt, and pepper. Add the noodles and then bring to a boil over high heat. Reduce heat to medium-high and simmer 15 minutes, or until noodles are done. Makes 5–6 servings.

TACO SOUP

16	**frozen, fully cooked meatballs,** thawed
1 can (14.5 ounces)	**diced tomatoes with garlic and onion,** with liquid
1 can (15.25 ounces)	**whole kernel corn,** drained
1 can (15 ounces)	**black or kidney beans,** rinsed and drained
1 can (8 ounces)	**tomato sauce**
2 cups	**water**
1 envelope	**taco seasoning**

Cut meatballs in half and place in a 3- to 4-quart soup pan. Stir in the remaining ingredients and bring to a boil. Lower to medium heat and simmer for 20 minutes, stirring occasionally. Makes 5–6 servings.

VARIATION: This soup can be served over crushed tortilla chips, and garnished with cheese and a dollop of sour cream.

SOUTHWESTERN CILANTRO RICE SOUP

4 cans (14 ounces each)	**beef broth**
2 cans (14.5 ounces each)	**diced tomatoes and green chiles,** with liquid
26 (1 pound)	**frozen, fully cooked meatballs**
1 cup	**chopped onion**
½ cup	**chopped fresh cilantro**
2 teaspoons	**Italian seasoning**
½ cup	**uncooked long-grain rice**
	grated Mexican-blend cheese, optional

In a 5- to 7-quart slow cooker prepared with nonstick cooking spray, stir together broth, tomatoes, meatballs, onion, cilantro, and seasoning. Sprinkle rice evenly over the soup. Cover and cook over high heat for 3–4 hours or on low heat for 6–8 hours. Garnish with cheese. Makes 10–12 servings.

NOTE: Recipe can be halved and prepared in a 3- to 4-quart slow cooker.

MEATBALL CHOWDER

13	**frozen, fully cooked meatballs,** thawed and sliced in half
2 cups	**frozen corn**
2$\frac{1}{2}$ cups	**water**
1 pound	**baking potatoes,** peeled and cut into $\frac{1}{2}$-inch pieces
$\frac{1}{2}$ tablespoon	**Old Bay seafood seasoning**
1 cup	**half-and-half**
$\frac{1}{2}$ cup	**grated sharp cheddar cheese**

In a 4-quart soup pan, combine meatball halves, corn, water, potatoes, and seasoning over high heat and bring to a boil. Cover and reduce heat. Simmer for 10 minutes, or until potatoes are done. Turn off the heat and then stir half-and-half into the soup. Ladle into individual bowls, sprinkle cheese over top, and serve. Makes 4–6 servings.

CHINESE BEEF NOODLE SOUP

1	**medium white onion,** thinly sliced
1 tablespoon	**olive oil**
1 teaspoon	**minced garlic**
1 tablespoon	**thinly sliced fresh ginger or 2 teaspoons dried ginger**
4 cans (14 ounces each)	**vegetable broth**
3 1/2 cups	**water**
3 tablespoons	**soy sauce**
1 teaspoon	**Chinese five-spice powder**
1 teaspoon	**paprika**
26 (1 pound)	**frozen, fully cooked meatballs**
1 package (6 ounces)	**uncooked chow mein stir-fry noodles**
2 tablespoons	**chopped fresh cilantro,** optional

In a 5- to 7-quart stockpot, saute onion in oil over high heat until translucent. Stir in garlic and ginger and cook for 1 minute. Pour in broth, water, and soy sauce. Stir in Chinese five-spice and paprika. Bring broth to a boil and then stir in meatballs and return to a boil. Lower heat to medium-high and simmer for 7–8 minutes. Stir in noodles and boil 6–10 minutes more. Garnish with cilantro. Makes 7–9 servings.

WINTER STEW

3	**medium potatoes,** peeled and cubed
I bag (16 ounces)	**baby carrots,** cut into thirds
2 to 3 stalks	**celery,** sliced
$^1/_2$	**medium onion,** chopped
26 (1 pound)	**frozen, fully cooked meatballs**
3 cups	**water**
I envelope	**beef stew seasoning mix**
I can (10.5 ounces)	**cream of mushroom soup,** condensed

In a 5- to 7-quart slow cooker prepared with nonstick cooking spray, layer potatoes, carrots, celery, onion, and meatballs.

In a bowl, combine water, stew mix, and soup. Pour mixture over meatball layer. Cover and cook on high heat for 4–5 hours or on low heat for 8–10 hours. Makes 8–10 servings.

CROWD-PLEASING MEATBALL CHILI

1	**medium onion,** chopped
1 tablespoon	**olive oil**
2 teaspoons	**minced garlic**
1 can (28 ounces)	**diced tomatoes,** with liquid
1 can (28 ounces)	**crushed tomatoes**
4 cans (16 ounces each)	**chili beans in sauce,** with liquid
1 can (4 ounces)	**diced green chiles**
1 to 2 tablespoons	**chili powder**
39 (1 ½ pounds)	**frozen, fully cooked meatballs,** thawed

In a 6- to 8-quart stockpot, saute onion in oil until translucent. Stir in remaining ingredients. Bring to a boil, stirring frequently. Simmer over medium-low heat for 20 minutes, stirring occasionally. Makes 14–16 servings.

WHITE BEAN SALSA CHILI

18	**frozen, fully cooked meatballs**
1 jar (16 ounces)	**chunky salsa**
1 can (15.25 ounces)	**white kernel corn,** with liquid
2 cans (15.5 ounces each)	**Great Northern beans,** drained and rinsed
1 can (14.5 ounces)	**diced tomatoes with green chiles,** with liquid

Combine all ingredients in a 3- to 5-quart slow cooker prepared with nonstick cooking spray. Cover and cook on high heat for 3 hours or on low heat for 6–8 hours. Makes 6 servings.

VARIATION: Defrost meatballs. Combine all ingredients in a 3 1/2- to 4-quart soup pan. Bring to a boil on the stovetop. Reduce heat and simmer for 15–20 minutes, stirring occasionally.

VARIATION: To add more heat to the chili, stir in 2 to 3 teaspoons chili powder.

MEATBALL ZUCCHINI ORZO SOUP

26 (I pound)	**frozen, fully cooked meatballs,** thawed
I	**small zucchini,** shredded
4 cans (14.5 ounces each)	**chicken broth**
I cup	**uncooked orzo pasta**
I teaspoon	**ground black pepper**
I teaspoon	**dried parsley flakes**
1/4 cup	**freshly squeezed lemon juice**
2	**eggs**

In a 4-quart soup pan, combine meatballs and zucchini. Add the broth, orzo, pepper, and parsley and bring to a boil. Reduce heat to medium-low and simmer uncovered 25–30 minutes.

In a separate bowl, beat together lemon juice and eggs. Stir 1/4 cup of the hot soup into the egg mixture. Pour egg mixture into the pot and simmer 2 minutes more. Serve immediately. Makes 6–8 servings.

CHEESY RICE AND HAMBURGER SOUP

26 (1 pound)	**frozen, fully cooked meatballs,** thawed
2 cans (10.5 ounces each)	**cheddar cheese soup,** condensed
2 cans (10.5 ounces each)	**tomato soup,** condensed
1 cup	**uncooked long-grain white rice**
3 1/2 cups	**water**
1/2 envelope	**dry onion soup mix**

Cut meatballs into quarters; set aside.

In a 4-quart soup pan, combine soups, rice, water, and dry soup mix over high heat. Stirring constantly, bring to a boil. Reduce to medium heat and then stir in meatballs. Cover and cook over medium heat for 30 minutes, stirring every 3–4 minutes to prevent rice from sticking to bottom of pan. Garnish with crushed saltine crackers and grated cheddar cheese if desired. Makes 6–8 servings.

GARDEN VEGGIE SOUP WITH BOW TIE PASTA

26 (1 pound)	**frozen, fully cooked meatballs**
1 can (14.5 ounces)	**diced tomatoes with garlic and onion,** with liquid
1/2 tablespoon	**dried basil**
1 box (32 ounces)	**beef or chicken broth**
1 cup	**water**
3	**carrots,** peeled and sliced
1	**medium summer squash,** cut in half lengthwise and sliced
1	**medium zucchini,** cut in half lengthwise and sliced
1	**medium red or green bell pepper,** seeded and chopped
1 1/2 cups	**uncooked bow tie pasta**

In a 5- to 7-quart slow cooker, combine all ingredients except pasta. Cover and cook on high heat for 3 1/2–4 hours or on low heat for 7–9 hours. During the last half hour of cooking, cook bow tie pasta according to package directions; drain pasta and add to soup. Serve immediately. Makes 8–10 servings.

SANDWICHES, WRAPS, & MORE

PHILLY MEATBALL SUB SANDWICHES

2	**green or red bell peppers,** sliced fajita style
1	**medium yellow onion,** sliced fajita style
1 tablespoon	**olive oil**
16	**frozen, fully cooked meatballs**
2 tablespoons	**Worcestershire sauce**
$^1/_2$ cup	**Heinz 57 sauce**
4	**hoagie rolls,** split and lightly toasted
4 slices	**provolone cheese**

In a frying pan, saute bell peppers and onion in oil until tender and starting to brown. While vegetables are cooking, place meatballs in a microwave-safe bowl with 1–2 tablespoons water. Microwave on high for 4 minutes, stirring halfway through. Drain any excess liquid.

In a small bowl, combine the sauces. Stir mixture into the meatballs. Divide sauteed vegetables over rolls. Evenly divide hot meatballs and cheese over top. Serve immediately. Makes 4 servings.

SAUCY MEATBALL GRINDERS

I jar (14 ounces)	**pizza sauce**
4 tablespoons	**apple jelly**
$1/2$ teaspoon	**Italian seasoning**
$1/2$ teaspoon	**salt**
$1/2$ teaspoon	**ground black pepper**
30	**frozen, fully cooked meatballs**
6	**hoagie rolls,** split lengthwise
I cup	**grated mozzarella cheese**

In a $2^1/2$- to 3-quart saucepan, combine pizza sauce, jelly, Italian seasoning, salt, and pepper. Bring to a slow boil over medium heat. Add meatballs to the sauce. Cover and simmer over medium heat for 18–20 minutes, stirring occasionally until meatballs are heated through. Reduce heat if sauce is too bubbly. During the last 10 minutes of cooking, preheat oven to 375 degrees. Place split hoagie rolls open face on a large baking sheet. Equally place meatballs on the bottom half of each roll. Drizzle desired amount of sauce over meatballs and sprinkle cheese over top. Bake uncovered for 2–3 minutes, or until cheese melts. Makes 6 servings.

CONEY MEATBALL SUBS

40	**frozen, fully cooked meatballs**
1	**medium onion,** peeled and quartered
1	**green bell pepper,** seeded and quartered
1 can (15 ounces)	**pork and beans**
1 can (10.75 ounces)	**tomato soup,** condensed
1 envelope	**taco seasoning**
1 tablespoon	**water**
	lettuce, torn
8 slices	**cheddar or pepper jack cheese**
8	**hoagie buns**

Place meatballs in a 3- to 4-quart slow cooker prepared with nonstick cooking spray.

In a blender or food processor, blend the onion and bell pepper. Add pork and beans, soup, seasoning, and water. Process until smooth and then pour mixture over meatballs. Cover and cook on low heat for 6–8 hours or on high heat for 3 1/2–4 hours. Layer lettuce, 5 meatballs, and a cheese slice on individual hoagie buns. Makes 8 servings.

VARIATION: For a spicier sauce, add chopped hot peppers or hot sauce to taste before cooking.

PESTO MEATBALL BAGUETTE SANDWICHES

¹/₄ cup	**pesto**
³/₄ cup	**mayonnaise**
¹/₂ tablespoon	**olive oil**
15	**cherry tomatoes,** sliced in half
25	**frozen, fully cooked meatballs,** thawed
5 (6-inch)	**baguettes,** split
	lettuce, torn into large pieces

In a bowl, combine pesto and mayonnaise. Refrigerate until ready to use. In a frying pan, heat the oil. Saute tomato halves in oil for 1–2 minutes. Add meatballs to pan and cook, stirring frequently, until meatballs are hot. Toast open-faced baguettes under broiler for 1–2 minutes or in a toaster oven. Spread mayonnaise mixture over both sides of baguettes. Spoon 5 meatballs evenly over each baguette. Add desired amount of lettuce and serve. Makes 5 sandwiches.

VARIATION: Hoagie buns can be used in place of baguettes.

PIPING HOT BUFFALO SUBS

25	**frozen, fully cooked meatballs**
1 jar (12–16 ounces)	**buffalo wing sauce**
5 (6-inch)	**hoagie or sub rolls**
	lettuce, torn into sandwich-size sections
10 thin slices	**tomato**
1	**medium red onion,** sliced
5 tablespoons	**chunky blue cheese dressing,** divided

Preheat oven to 400 degrees.

Place meatballs in an 8 x 8-inch pan. Pour buffalo wing sauce over meatballs and then cover with aluminum foil. Bake for 35 minutes, or until bubbly. Split rolls and broil open-faced on a baking sheet for 1–2 minutes, or until lightly toasted. Layer lettuce, 2 tomato slices, and red onion rings on rolls. Spoon 5 meatballs with desired amount of sauce on each sandwich. Spread 1 tablespoon dressing over top. Serve immediately. Makes 5 servings.

ROASTED PEPPER AND MEATBALLS ON RYE

18	**frozen, fully cooked meatballs**
I container (8 ounces)	**chive-and-onion cream cheese**
6 slices	**rye bread**
6 tablespoons	**jarred sweet roasted red peppers**
3	**romaine lettuce leaves,** torn to fit sandwich
6	**deep-fried onion rings,** plus more

Heat meatballs according to package directions. Spread desired amount of cream cheese over each slice of bread. Spoon 2 tablespoons roasted peppers over 3 slices of bread. Place 6 heated meatballs over pepper layer. Add a lettuce leaf, followed by 2 onion rings. Top with remaining bread slices, cream cheese side down. Serve immediately with additional onion rings. Makes 3 servings.

MEDITERRANEAN MEATBALL SANDWICHES

12	**frozen, fully cooked meatballs**
6 tablespoons	**sour cream**
1/2 teaspoon	**minced garlic**
6 slices	**multigrain or olive bread**
1/2 bag (8 ounces)	**Mediterranean-blend salad**
3 slices	**red onion**
4 1/2 tablespoons	**grated Parmesan cheese**

Heat meatballs according to package directions and then cut each into 3 slices. Combine sour cream and garlic. Spread 1 tablespoon sour cream mixture over each slice of bread. Place a layer of salad over 3 pieces of bread. Layer the hot meatball slices, red onion, and Parmesan cheese over the top. Top with remaining bread, sour cream side down. Serve immediately with any remaining salad on the side. Makes 3 servings.

ITALIAN FOCACCIA MEATBALL SANDWICHES

9	**frozen, fully cooked meatballs**
2 tablespoons	**water**
I rectangle (12 ounces)	**focaccia bread**
3 tablespoons	**olive oil**
6 tablespoons	**warm spaghetti sauce**
3 tablespoons	**jarred sun-dried tomato pieces,** drained and julienned
3/4 cup	**grated mozzarella cheese**
3	**fresh basil leaves,** chopped

In a microwave-safe bowl, microwave meatballs with the water on high for 3 minutes, or until hot. Cut meatballs in half; set aside.

Cut bread into 3 equal sections. Turn each piece on end and slice in half. Place the 6 slices cut side up on a baking sheet. Brush oil over top. Broil on high for 1–2 minutes, or until lightly toasted. Spoon 2 tablespoons spaghetti sauce over 3 bottoms. Sprinkle 1 tablespoon sun-dried tomatoes over sauce. Lay 6 meatball halves evenly over each bottom. Sprinkle 1/4 cup cheese evenly over each meatball layer. Broil for 1–2 minutes more, or until cheese melts. Sprinkle one-third of the basil over top. Place remaining toasted halves over each sandwich. Makes 3 servings.

SWEDISH MEATBALL HERO

30	**frozen, fully cooked meatballs**
2 jars (12 ounces each)	**brown beef gravy**
6 (6-inch)	**hoagie or hero rolls,** split

Preheat oven to 375 degrees.

Place frozen meatballs in an 8 x 8-inch pan. Pour gravy over the meatballs and cover the pan with aluminum foil. Bake 45–55 minutes, or until bubbly. Spoon 5 meatballs and desired amount of sauce inside each roll. Makes 6 sandwiches.

VARIATION: Bake meatballs and gravy following the instructions above. Serve over hot cooked noodles or mashed potatoes.

OPEN-FACED MEATBALL SUB

30	**frozen, fully cooked meatballs**
I jar (26 ounces)	**spaghetti or marinara sauce**
6	**hoagie or sub rolls,** split
I cup	**grated mozzarella cheese**

In a 2¹/₂- to 3-quart saucepan, combine meatballs and sauce. Bring to a boil, stirring occasionally; reduce heat. Cover and simmer for 10 minutes, or until meatballs are thoroughly heated. Spoon 5 meatballs and some sauce over each roll. Sprinkle cheese evenly over meatballs and serve immediately. Makes 6 servings.

VARIATION: Sub rolls can be toasted in a toaster oven or broiled in a regular oven for 2 minutes before topping with meatballs and cheese.

FALL CRANBERRY WRAP

10	**frozen, fully cooked meatballs**
2 (10-inch)	**flour tortillas**
4 tablespoons	**whole cranberry sauce,** divided
4 tablespoons	**grated sharp cheddar cheese**
6	**thin apple slices**
	sprouts, optional

In a microwave, heat meatballs in a microwave-safe bowl in 1 tablespoon water on high for 1 1/2–2 minutes, or until meatballs are hot. Place 5 meatballs down the center of each tortilla. Spread 2 tablespoons cranberry sauce alongside the meatballs. Sprinkle cheese evenly over top. Place 3 apple slices down center of each tortilla, as well as the sprouts. Roll or wrap burrito-style and then serve immediately. Makes 2 servings.

YUMMY STUFFED PITAS

9	**frozen, fully cooked meatballs**
1/2 teaspoon	**minced garlic**
1/2 container (8 ounces)	**plain yogurt**
3	**pita bread pockets, warmed**
I	**Roma tomato,** diced
1/2 cup	**shredded lettuce**
3 tablespoons	**crumbled feta cheese,** any variety
3 tablespoons	**sliced black olives**
3 tablespoons	**chopped red onion**

Heat meatballs according to package directions. Stir garlic into yogurt. Place 3 heated meatballs in each pita pocket. Fill pitas with tomato, lettuce, cheese, olives, and onion. Spoon desired amount of garlic yogurt sauce over top. Makes 3 pitas.

EASY SLOPPY JOES

39 (1 ½ pounds)	**frozen, fully cooked meatballs,** thawed
1 ¼ cups	**ketchup**
1 tablespoon	**dried minced onion**
1 tablespoon	**sugar**
2 tablespoons	**yellow mustard**
1 tablespoon	**apple cider vinegar**
8	**large hamburger buns**

Crumble meatballs using a food processor or by hand. In a frying pan, saute crumbled meatballs for 5–8 minutes over medium-high heat stirring frequently. Stir in ketchup, dried onion, sugar, mustard, and vinegar. Reduce heat to medium-low. Cover and simmer for 25 minutes, stirring occasionally. Serve on warmed buns. Makes 8 servings.

DRESSED-UP MEATBALLS

CROWD-PLEASING MEATBALLS

1 cup	**grape juice**
1 cup	**apple jelly**
1 cup	**ketchup**
1 cup	**spicy barbecue sauce**
1 can (8 ounces)	**tomato sauce**
2 teaspoons	**crushed red chili pepper flakes**
104 (4 pounds)	**frozen, fully cooked meatballs**

In a 2-quart saucepan, combine juice, jelly, ketchup, barbecue sauce, tomato sauce, and crushed pepper flakes. Heat over medium heat until jelly is melted into the sauce. Place meatballs in a 5-quart slow cooker prepared with nonstick cooking spray. Pour sauce evenly over meatballs. Cover and cook on low heat for 4–6 hours. Serve as an appetizer with toothpicks. Makes 25–30 servings.

VARIATION: This recipe can also be turned into a main dish by serving over a bed of rice with grated Swiss cheese sprinkled over top.

NOTE: This recipe can be halved and cooked on low heat for 4–6 hours in a 3-quart slow cooker.

MARINATED MEATBALLS

39 (1 1/2 pounds)	**frozen, fully cooked meatballs**
3 cups	**beef or vegetable broth**
1/2 teaspoon	**lemon zest**
1 teaspoon	**lemon juice**
1 tablespoon	**dried parsley flakes**
1/2 teaspoon	**paprika**
1/2 teaspoon	**fresh grated nutmeg**
1/4 teaspoon	**ground allspice**

Place the meatballs in an 8-cup-capacity plastic bowl that has a tight lid. In a saucepan, combine the remaining ingredients. Bring the broth mixture to a boil. Lower temperature to medium and simmer for 15 minutes. Pour mixture over meatballs. Cover and refrigerate for 24 hours or more. Place the meatballs and marinade in a large frying pan and bring to a boil; boil 10 minutes and then remove meatballs to a serving dish. Boil sauce 5 minutes more, or until thickened. Pour sauce over meatballs. Serve as an appetizer with toothpicks or over buttered egg noodles. Makes 6–8 servings.

SWEET AND
SPICY MEATBALLS

1 can (16 ounces)	**jellied cranberry sauce**
1 jar (10 ounces)	**chili sauce**
1 tablespoon	**brown sugar**
1 tablespoon	**lemon juice**
52 (2 pounds)	**frozen, fully cooked meatballs,**
	thawed

In a 4-quart saucepan, combine cranberry sauce, chili sauce, brown sugar, and lemon juice. Cook over medium-high heat stirring frequently until cranberry sauce melts and sauce is mostly smooth. Stir in meatballs. Simmer over medium heat for 10–15 minutes, or until meatballs are hot. Serve as an appetizer with toothpicks or over hot cooked rice as a main dish. Makes 10 servings.

CRANBERRY SAUERKRAUT MEATBALLS

I can (14.5 ounces)	**sauerkraut,** with liquid
I can (16 ounces)	**jellied cranberry sauce**
¹/₂ cup	**packed brown sugar**
¹/₂ jar (26 ounces)	**spaghetti sauce with onion and garlic**
78 (3 pounds)	**frozen, fully cooked meatballs**

In a bowl, combine sauerkraut, cranberry sauce, brown sugar, and spaghetti sauce. Place the meatballs in a 4- to 6-quart slow cooker prepared with nonstick cooking spray. Spoon sauerkraut mixture evenly over meatballs. Cover and cook on low heat for 4–6 hours, or until fully heated. Serve with toothpicks as an appetizer or over hot cooked pasta as a main dish. Makes 12–16 servings.

ITALIAN-STYLE COCKTAIL MEATBALLS

39 (1 1/2 pounds)	**frozen, fully cooked meatballs**
1/3 cup	**packed brown sugar**
2 cans (8 ounces each)	**tomato sauce**
1/2 cup	**red wine or apple cider vinegar**

In a 2- to 3-quart pan, combine tomato sauce, brown sugar, and vinegar. Fold in meatballs. Cover and bring to a low boil. Reduce heat to medium and simmer for 15–20 minutes, stirring occasionally. Serve as an appetizer with toothpicks or over hot cooked angel hair pasta. Makes 7–9 servings.

BLUE CHEESE BUFFALO BALLS

30	**frozen, fully cooked meatballs**
I jar (12–16 ounces)	**buffalo wing sauce**
I bottle (12 ounces)	**chunky blue cheese dressing**

Preheat oven to 375 degrees.

Place meatballs in an 8 x 8-inch pan and pour buffalo wing sauce over top. Cover pan with aluminum foil. Bake for 45–50 minutes, or until bubbly. Serve with toothpicks and blue cheese dressing on the side for dipping. Makes 6–7 servings.

SPORTS DAY MEATBALLS

2 jars (12 ounces each)	**chili sauce**
2 tablespoons	**water,** divided
1 1/2 cups	**grape jelly**
60 (2 1/4 pounds)	**frozen, fully cooked meatballs**

Pour chili sauce into a 3- to 5-quart slow cooker that has been prepared with nonstick cooking spray. Add 1 tablespoon water to each jar, then replace the lid and shake the jar to release the chili sauce from sides of jar; pour remaining sauce into slow cooker. Stir grape jelly into chili sauce mixture. Add meatballs to slow cooker and stir to coat. Cover and cook on low heat for 4–6 hours, or until meatballs are heated through. Serve as an appetizer with toothpicks. Makes 12–15 servings.

VARIATION: Combine all ingredients in a 3- to 5-quart saucepan. Cover and simmer over medium-low heat on the stove for 50–55 minutes, stirring occasionally until meatballs are heated through. Serve in a chafing dish to keep warm during a party.

MAGNIFICENT MEATBALLS

52 (2 pounds)	**frozen, fully cooked meatballs**
I jar (18 ounces)	**apricot preserves**
I jar (16 ounces)	**medium salsa**
I tablespoon	**cinnamon**

Place meatballs in a 3- to 4½-quart slow cooker that has been prepared with nonstick cooking spray. In a bowl, combine the remaining ingredients. Pour sauce over meatballs. Cover and cook on low heat for 4–6 hours, or until meatballs are heated through. Serve as an appetizer with toothpicks or over rice as a main dish. Makes 10–12 servings.

VARIATION: Combine all ingredients in a 3- to 4-quart saucepan. Cover and simmer over medium-low heat on the stove for 55–60 minutes, stirring occasionally until meatballs are heated through.

SAUCY MEATBALLS

1 cup	**ketchup**
2 tablespoons	**apple cider vinegar**
2 tablespoons	**Worcestershire sauce**
1 tablespoon	**sugar**
$1/2$ teaspoon	**onion powder**
$1/2$ teaspoon	**minced garlic**
26 (1 pound)	**frozen, fully cooked meatballs,** thawed

In a saucepan, combine ketchup, vinegar, Worcestershire, sugar, onion powder, and garlic. Simmer over medium heat until bubbly. Stir meatballs into the sauce. Cover and cook over medium-low heat 15–20 minutes, stirring occasionally until meatballs are heated through. Serve as an appetizer with toothpicks or on hoagie buns with Monterey Jack cheese. Makes 5–6 servings.

TERIYAKI MEATBALLS

39 (1 ½ pounds)	**frozen, fully cooked meatballs**
I can (8 ounces)	**crushed pineapple,** with liquid
I jar (20 ounces)	**teriyaki sauce**

Place frozen meatballs in a 2½- to 3½-quart slow cooker prepared with nonstick cooking spray. Spoon pineapple evenly over meatballs and pour teriyaki sauce over top. Cover and cook on low heat for 6–8 hours or on high heat for 3 hours. Serve as an appetizer with toothpicks or over hot cooked rice. Makes 7–9 servings.

VARIATION: Defrost meatballs. In a 3- to 4-quart saucepan, combine teriyaki sauce and crushed pineapple. Bring to a low boil stirring constantly. Stir in thawed meatballs. Simmer over medium heat for 10–15 minutes, stirring frequently, until meatballs are heated.

MAPLE MEATBALLS

½ cup	**real maple syrup**
½ cup	**chili sauce**
2 teaspoons	**dried chives** (or 2 tablespoons fresh chives)
1 tablespoon	**soy sauce**
½ teaspoon	**ground mustard**
26 (1 pound)	**frozen, fully cooked meatballs,** thawed

In a saucepan, combine syrup, chili sauce, chives, soy sauce, and ground mustard. Bring to a low boil. Add meatballs and then return to a boil. Simmer over medium heat for 8–10 minutes, stirring occasionally until meatballs are thoroughly heated. Serve as an appetizer with toothpicks or over hot cooked rice. Makes 5–6 servings.

FETA MEATBALLS WITH CUCUMBER YOGURT SAUCE

26 (1 pound)	**frozen, fully cooked meatballs**
1 container (4 ounces)	**crumbled tomato basil feta cheese**

Cucumber Yogurt Sauce:

1 1/2 cups	**nonfat plain yogurt**
4 ounces	**low-fat cream cheese**
1/2 cup	**diced seedless cucumber**
1 teaspoon	**minced garlic**
1 1/2 teaspoons	**dried dill seasoning**
1 teaspoon	**fresh lemon juice**
1 teaspoon	**lemon zest**

Preheat oven to 375 degrees. Place meatballs in the bottom of an 8 x 8-inch pan with 1/2 inch of water and bake 40 minutes. While meatballs cook, place all yogurt sauce ingredients in a blender or food processor and blend until smooth. Pour the sauce in a bowl for dipping and refrigerate until ready to serve. Place baked meatballs on a serving platter and sprinkle with the cheese. Serve immediately with toothpicks and the yogurt sauce on the side. Makes 4–6 servings.

SPICY JAMAICAN JERK MEATBALLS

39 (1 1/2 pounds)	**frozen, fully cooked meatballs,** thawed

Jerk Seasoning:

1 tablespoon	**brown sugar**
1 teaspoon	**ground allspice**
1 teaspoon	**ground cinnamon**
1/2 teaspoon	**ground ginger**
1/2 teaspoon	**onion powder**
1/2 teaspoon	**garlic powder**
1/2 teaspoon	**ground black pepper**
1/4 teaspoon	**cayenne pepper**
1/4 teaspoon	**ground cloves**

Jerk Sauce:

1/2 cup	**ketchup**
2/3 cup	**honey**
1 tablespoon	**Jamaican jerk seasoning**
1 cup	**white vinegar**

Preheat oven to 375 degrees.

Place meatballs in a gallon-size ziplock bag. In a bowl, combine all jerk seasoning ingredients. Pour seasoning over meatballs. Seal bag and shake well to cover.

In a saucepan, combine jerk sauce ingredients and bring to a boil. Place meatballs in a 7 x 11-inch pan prepared with nonstick cooking spray. Pour sauce over the top and then cover pan with aluminum foil. Bake for 35–40 minutes. Serve as an appetizer with toothpicks or over hot cooked rice. Makes 8–10 servings.

ASIAN MEATBALL APPETIZERS

1 bottle (18 ounces)	**honey barbecue sauce**
1 can (8 ounces)	**crushed pineapple,** with liquid
1 ½ teaspoons	**sugar**
26 (1 pound)	**frozen, fully cooked meatballs,** thawed

Preheat oven to 350 degrees.

In a bowl, combine barbecue sauce, pineapple, and sugar. Place meatballs in a deep 8 x 8-inch baking dish and pour sauce over top. Bake uncovered for 35–40 minutes, or until bubbly. Serve as an appetizer with toothpicks or over hot cooked rice garnished with crunchy chow mien noodles. Makes 6–8 servings.

GINGER ALE MEATBALLS

39 (1 1/2 pounds)	**frozen, fully cooked meatballs**
2 cups	**ginger ale**
2 cups	**ketchup**
1 teaspoon	**minced garlic**

Place frozen meatballs in a 3- to 4-quart slow cooker prepared with nonstick cooking spray.

In a bowl, combine ginger ale, ketchup, and garlic. Pour mixture over meatballs. Cover and cook on low heat for 6–8 hours or on high heat for 3 hours. Serve with toothpicks as an appetizer, on hoagie buns, or over hot cooked noodles. Makes 8–10 servings.

CHEESY MEATBALLS

26 (1 pound)	**frozen, fully cooked meatballs**
$^1/_2$ cup	**water**
1 jar (15 ounces)	**Cheez Whiz**
	sliced green onions, optional

Place frozen meatballs in a 2-quart pan and drizzle the water over top. Bring to a boil. Cover and simmer for 8–10 minutes over medium-high heat, stirring occasionally. Pour Cheese Whiz into a microwave-safe bowl and microwave on high heat for 2–3 minutes, stirring occasionally until cheese is melted. Fold melted cheese dip into meatballs. Serve with toothpicks or individually over snack crackers. Garnish with green onion. Makes 26 appetizers.

NOTE: 1 jar (16 ounces) Ragu cheese sauce can be used in place of Cheez Whiz.

SALSA VERDE MEATBALLS

39 (1 ½ pounds)	**frozen, fully cooked meatballs**
1 jar (16 ounces)	**salsa verde**
1	**medium onion,** chopped
2 teaspoons	**minced garlic**
½ cup	**chicken or beef broth**
½ teaspoon	**ground cumin**

Place frozen meatballs in a 3- to 4-quart slow cooker prepared with nonstick cooking spray.

In a bowl, combine the remaining ingredients. Pour mixture over meatballs. Cover and cook on high heat for 3 hours or on low heat for 6–8 hours. Serve as an appetizer with tortilla chips or toothpicks or in a tortilla with beans and rice. Makes 6–8 servings.

VARIATION: Defrost meatballs. In a 3 ½- to 4-quart pan, combine the remaining ingredients and bring to a low boil. Stir in meatballs. Return to a low boil. Simmer over medium heat for 15 minutes.

HOLIDAY MEATBALLS

52 (2 pounds)	**frozen, fully cooked meatballs**
I can (16 ounces)	**whole berry cranberry sauce**
I cup	**barbecue sauce**

Place frozen meatballs in a 3$\frac{1}{2}$- to 5-quart slow cooker prepared with nonstick cooking spray.

In a bowl, stir together cranberry sauce and barbecue sauce. Pour mixture over meatballs. Cover and cook on low heat for 5–6 hours or on high heat for 2$\frac{1}{2}$–3 hours. During a party, meatballs can be left in the slow cooker on the warm or low setting. Serve as appetizers with toothpicks.

VARIATION: Combine all ingredients in a 3- to 4-quart saucepan. Cover and simmer over medium-low heat on the stove for 55–60 minutes, stirring occasionally until meatballs are heated through.

SOUR CREAM-SAUCED MEATBALLS

1 container (16 ounces)	**sour cream**
1 envelope	**dry onion soup mix**
26 (1 pound)	**frozen, fully cooked meatballs,** thawed

In a 2- to 3-quart pan, combine sour cream and dry soup mix. Stir in meatballs. Bring to a low boil. Reduce heat to medium and simmer for 10 minutes, stirring occasionally until meatballs are heated through. Serve as an appetizer with toothpicks, over hot cooked pasta, or over mashed potatoes. Makes 5–6 servings.

PASTA
DINNERS

MEATBALL
FETTUCCINE ALFREDO

1/2 tablespoon	**olive oil**
1/2 teaspoon	**salt**
1 box (12 ounces)	**fettuccine pasta**
1 jar (16 ounces)	**alfredo sauce**
20	**frozen, fully-cooked meatballs,** thawed
2 tablespoons	**chopped fresh parsley**

In a 4- to 6-quart stockpot, bring 4 quarts water, oil, and salt to a boil. Add pasta and cook according to directions.

In a separate saucepan, combine alfredo sauce and meatballs and bring to a boil. Lower heat and cover. Simmer for 10 minutes, stirring occasionally. Drain pasta and then place noodles on a large serving platter. Spoon meatballs and sauce evenly over top. Garnish with the parsley and serve. Makes 6 servings.

CHIPOTLE MEATBALL PASTA

I can (29 ounces)	**tomato sauce**
I can (28 ounces)	**crushed tomatoes**
I tablespoon	**onion powder**
I teaspoon	**minced garlic**
1/2 teaspoon	**cinnamon**
1/2 teaspoon	**oregano**
1/4 cup	**chopped chipotle honey-roasted green chiles**
26 (I pound)	**frozen, fully cooked meatballs**
9 cups	**hot cooked pasta**
	grated Parmesan or Monterey Jack cheese

In a 4-quart saucepan, combine tomato sauce, tomatoes, onion powder, garlic, cinnamon, oregano, and chiles over medium-high heat. Once bubbly, add the meatballs. Bring mixture to a low boil. Cover and reduce to medium heat. Simmer for 20–25 minutes, stirring occasionally. Serve over pasta and garnish with cheese. Makes 6 servings.

VARIATION: If you cannot find jarred chopped chipotle chiles, you can use a can of chipotle peppers in adobo sauce found in the Hispanic food section of your grocery store. Chop 4 peppers and toss them into the sauce.

FLORENTINE MEATBALLS AND NOODLES

½ package (10 ounces)	**frozen chopped spinach,** partially thawed
1 can (10.5 ounces)	**cream of mushroom soup,** condensed
½ cup	**butter or margarine**
1 cup	**heavy whipping cream**
1 can (4 ounces)	**sliced mushrooms,** drained
26 (1 pound)	**frozen, fully cooked meatballs,** thawed
⅓ cup	**grated Parmesan cheese**
8 cups	**hot cooked egg noodles**

In a 3- to 4-quart saucepan, cook spinach and soup over medium heat until spinach is heated. Stir in butter, cream, and mushrooms until butter is completely melted. Add meatballs to the sauce. Simmer over medium heat for 6–8 minutes, stirring every 2–3 minutes to assure the sauce doesn't burn. Stir in the cheese until it melts and then pour the sauce over the noodles. Serve immediately. Makes 6–8 servings.

MEATBALLS IN BLUE CHEESE SAUCE

1/4 cup	**butter or margarine**
I teaspoon	**minced garlic**
4 tablespoons	**flour**
I can (14.5 ounces)	**chicken broth**
I cup	**half-and-half**
I container (5 ounces)	**crumbled blue cheese**
39 (1 1/2 pounds)	**frozen, fully cooked meatballs,** thawed
1/4 cup	**chopped fresh parsley**
8 to 10 cups	**hot cooked pasta**

In a 3-quart saucepan, melt butter over medium-high heat. Saute garlic in butter for I minute. Stir in flour until completely blended. Gradually mix broth into flour mixture until completely dissolved. Stir in half-and-half and heat until sauce begins to bubble. Stir in blue cheese until melted. Add meatballs and then reduce heat to medium. Cover and simmer for 15 minutes, stirring occasionally, until meatballs are heated through. Sprinkle parsley over the sauce and serve over pasta or mashed potatoes. Makes 8–10 servings.

VARIATION: Use 52 (2 pounds) meatballs with the sauce. Serve with toothpicks as an appetizer in a chafing dish with cooked, crumbled bacon sprinkled over the top.

SLOW-COOKED TOMATO SOUP MEATBALLS

26 (1 pound)	**frozen, fully cooked meatballs**
¹/₂ cup	**chopped white onion**
¹/₃ cup	**chopped green bell pepper**
1 can (10.5 ounces)	**tomato soup,** condensed
2 tablespoons	**brown sugar**
1 tablespoon	**apple cider vinegar**
1 tablespoon	**Worcestershire sauce**
1 teaspoon	**mustard**
6 to 8 cups	**hot cooked linguine or rotini pasta**

Place meatballs in a 3- to 4-quart slow cooker prepared with nonstick cooking spray. Sprinkle onion and bell pepper over meatballs.

In a bowl, combine soup, brown sugar, vinegar, Worcestershire, and mustard. Pour sauce over meatballs and vegetables. Cover and cook on low heat for 6–8 hours or on high heat for 3 hours. Serve over the pasta. Makes 5–6 servings.

EASY MEATBALL LASAGNA

26 (1 pound)	**frozen, fully cooked meatballs,** thawed and halved or quartered
2 jars (26 ounces each)	**spaghetti sauce,** divided
3/4 cup	**water,** divided
1	**egg,** beaten
1 container (15 ounces)	**ricotta cheese**
2 cups	**grated mozzarella cheese,** divided
1 box (12 ounces)	**oven-ready lasagna noodles,** uncooked
1/2 cup	**grated Parmesan cheese**

Preheat oven to 400 degrees.

Place meatballs in a large bowl. Reserve 2 1/2 cups spaghetti sauce, and then pour the remaining over meatballs and stir in 1/2 cup water.

In a separate bowl, combine the egg, ricotta cheese, and 1 cup mozzarella cheese. Spread 1 cup of the reserved sauce in a 9 x 13-inch pan prepared with nonstick cooking spray. Lay 5 to 6 noodles over sauce and spread half the cheese mixture over the noodles. Spoon half the meatball mixture over the cheese. Repeat layers once. Add a final layer of noodles and spoon remaining sauce over top. Drizzle remaining water over top. Cover with heavy-duty aluminum foil. Bake for 55–60 minutes. Sprinkle Parmesan cheese over top and bake, uncovered, 5 minutes more. Let stand 5 minutes before serving. Makes 8 servings.

PESTO SPAGHETTI AND MEATBALLS

I package (16 ounces)	**spaghetti**
20	**frozen, fully cooked meatballs**
I jar (26 ounces)	**spaghetti sauce**
I jar (6–7 ounces)	**pesto**
I cup	**grated mozzarella cheese**

Cook spaghetti according to package directions. While water for spaghetti heats to a boil, combine meatballs and spaghetti sauce in a 2- to 3-quart saucepan and bring to a boil, stirring occasionally; reduce heat. Cover and simmer for 8–10 minutes. Drain spaghetti. Stir pesto into cooked spaghetti. Spoon sauce and hot meatballs over the pesto noodles and sprinkle cheese over top. Makes 5 servings.

RICOTTA-STUFFED SHELLS AND MEATBALLS

8	**frozen ricotta cheese–stuffed shell pasta**
26 (1 pound)	**frozen, fully cooked meatballs,** thawed
1 jar (26 ounces)	**spaghetti sauce**
1 ¼ cups	**grated Italian-blend cheese**

Preheat oven to 400 degrees.

Arrange pasta and meatballs in a 9 x 13-inch pan prepared with nonstick cooking spray. Pour spaghetti sauce evenly over top. Sprinkle cheese over sauce. Cover with aluminum foil and bake for 35–40 minutes. Uncover and bake 5 minutes more, or until cheese is melted. Makes 6–8 servings.

BAKED ZITI AND MEATBALLS

20	**frozen, fully cooked meatballs**
I package (16 ounces)	**ziti or other pasta**
I jar (26 ounces)	**spaghetti sauce**
2 cups	**grated mozzarella cheese,** divided
	chopped fresh basil or parsley, optional

Preheat oven to 350 degrees.

Heat meatballs according to package directions. Cook pasta according to package directions and drain. Stir in the spaghetti sauce, meatballs, and half the cheese. Place pasta mixture in a 9 x 13-inch pan prepared with nonstick cooking spray. Bake for 20 minutes. Sprinkle remaining cheese over top and bake 5 minutes more. Garnish with the basil or parsley if desired. Makes 8 servings.

EGGPLANT PARMESAN

1	**large eggplant,** peeled and diced
2 teaspoons	**minced garlic**
1 teaspoon	**Italian seasoning**
1 jar (26 ounces)	**spaghetti sauce**
30	**frozen, fully cooked meatballs,** thawed
1 cup	**seasoned breadcrumbs**
1/2 cup	**grated Parmesan cheese**
8 to 10 cups	**hot cooked pasta**

Place eggplant in a 4- to 5-quart stockpot. Cover with water and bring to a boil, stirring occasionally. Reduce heat to cook at a low boil for 8 minutes, stirring frequently; drain.

Preheat oven to 350 degrees.

In a bowl, stir together the eggplant, garlic, Italian seasoning, spaghetti sauce, and meatballs. Pour into a 9 x 13-inch pan prepared with non-stick cooking spray.

In a separate bowl, combine the breadcrumbs and cheese. Sprinkle mixture evenly over the eggplant mixture. Bake for 30–35 minutes, or until bubbly and golden. Serve over the pasta. Makes 6–8 servings.

ITALIAN-TOSSED TORTELLINI

¹/₂ cup	**chopped red onion**
¹/₂ cup	**chopped red bell pepper**
¹/₂ cup	**chopped green bell pepper**
1 tablespoon	**olive oil**
20	**frozen, fully cooked meatballs,** thawed
2 bags (13 ounces each)	**frozen cheese tortellini**
1 bottle (16 ounces)	**Italian dressing**

In a large frying pan, saute the onion and bell peppers in hot oil for 3 minutes. Quarter meatballs and then add to the vegetables and cook 4 minutes more. Cook tortellini according to package directions. Drain tortellini and stir Italian dressing into pasta while still hot. Gently toss vegetable and meat mixture with the warm tortellini. Serve hot or cold. Makes 8 servings.

RAVIOLI MEATBALL STIR-FRY

2 tablespoons	**peanut or olive oil**
1 bag (16 ounces)	**frozen stir-fry vegetables**
13	**frozen, fully cooked meatballs,** thawed
1 bottle (12 ounces)	**stir-fry sauce**
1 bag (25 ounces)	**frozen cheese ravioli,** thawed

In a wok or stir-fry pan, heat oil until hot. Add frozen vegetables and stir-fry over high heat for 3 minutes. Stir in meatballs and cook 4 minutes more. Add the stir-fry sauce and toss in the ravioli. Stir-fry for 3–4 minutes, or until ravioli is heated through. Serve immediately. Makes 6 servings.

MEATBALL STROGANOFF

39 (1 ½ pounds)	**frozen, fully cooked meatballs**
2 cans (10.5 ounces each)	**cream of mushroom soup,** condensed
1 teaspoon	**Worcestershire sauce**
¼ cup	**water**
1 dash	**Tabasco sauce**
1 cup	**sour cream**
1 can (7 ounces)	**mushroom stems and pieces,** drained
8 to 10 cups	**hot cooked egg noodles**

Place meatballs in a 3- to 4½-quart slow cooker prepared with nonstick cooking spray.

In a medium bowl, combine the soup, Worcestershire, water, and Tabasco. Spoon mixture over the meatballs. Cover and cook on low heat for 4–4½ hours. Stir in sour cream and mushrooms. Cover and cook 30 minutes more. Serve over the egg noodles. Makes 8 servings.

VARIATION: Heat meatballs according to package directions for stovetop in a 4-quart saucepan. Drain any excess liquid. In a medium bowl, combine all remaining ingredients. Add soup mixture to meatballs. Simmer over medium heat for 20 minutes, stirring occasionally. Serve over egg noodles.

AMAZING
MEATBALL TORTELLINI

1/4 cup	**raisins**
2 tablespoons	**olive oil**
1/2 cup	**chopped onion**
1 cup	**jarred julienned sun-dried tomatoes,** drained
1 teaspoon	**crushed red pepper**
1/2 tablespoon	**minced garlic**
26 (1 pound)	**frozen, fully cooked meatballs,** thawed
2 cans (14.5 ounces each)	**diced tomatoes,** with liquid
1 bunch	**curly endive,** leaves only
2 bags (13 ounces each)	**frozen cheese tortellini,** thawed
1/3 cup	**pine nuts**

In a small bowl, soak raisins in some water for 25 minutes; set aside.

In a 5- to 6-quart soup pan, heat the oil. Saute the onion, sun-dried tomatoes, crushed red pepper, and garlic in the oil until onions are tender. Stir in meatballs and tomatoes. Simmer over medium-high heat for 5 minutes. Stir in the endive leaves and simmer 5 minutes more. Stir in drained raisins, tortellini, and pine nuts. Simmer over medium heat for 5–10 minutes, stirring occasionally, until tortellini is heated. Makes 8–10 servings.

VARIATION: Use 1 bag (9 ounces) spinach leaves in place of curly endive.

CHEESY BROCCOLI MEATBALLS

1 box (16 ounces)	**bow tie pasta**
26 (1 pound)	**frozen, fully cooked meatballs**
2 tablespoons	**water**
$^2/_3$ cup	**half-and-half**
2 boxes (10 ounces each)	**frozen broccoli with cheese sauce**

Cook pasta according to package directions; drain.

In a large frying pan, saute meatballs in the water over medium-high heat for 5–6 minutes. Stir in half-and-half. Place blocks of frozen broccoli and sauce in the frying pan, vegetable side down. Cover and cook 10–12 minutes, stirring occasionally, until vegetables are thoroughly heated. Serve over the pasta. Makes 6 servings.

VARIATION: This recipe can also be served over hot cooked rice.

DINNERS WITH RICE

EASY RICE AND MEATBALLS

26 (1 pound)	**frozen, fully cooked meatballs**
3 cups	**water**
1 envelope	**dry onion soup mix**
1/2 cup	**chopped white onion**
1/2 cup	**chopped green bell pepper**
1 can (4 ounces)	**mushroom pieces,** drained
1 can (14.5 ounces)	**petite-cut diced tomatoes,** with liquid
2 cups	**uncooked white long-grain rice**

In a 4-quart saucepan, combine meatballs, water, and dry soup mix, and bring to a boil. Simmer over medium-high heat for 8–10 minutes. Add the remaining ingredients and return to a boil. Reduce heat to medium-low. Stir and then cover and simmer for 25 minutes. Let cool for 5 minutes and then stir again right before serving. Makes 6 servings.

MEATBALLS IN CURRY SAUCE

2 tablespoons	**butter or margarine**
$^{1}/_{2}$ cup	**chopped red onion**
I teaspoon	**curry powder**
I can (10.5 ounces)	**cream of celery soup,** condensed
$^{1}/_{2}$ cup	**sour cream**
26 (I pound)	**frozen, fully cooked meatballs,** thawed
6 cups	**hot cooked rice**

In a 2$^{1}/_{2}$- to 3-quart saucepan, melt the butter. Stir in onion and saute until tender. Stir in curry powder and cook for I $^{1}/_{2}$–2 minutes. Stir in soup and sour cream. Return to a low simmer. Once bubbly, stir in meatballs. Cook over medium heat for 8–10 minutes, stirring often. Serve over rice. If desired, garnish with the shredded coconut and chopped peanuts. Makes 4–6 servings.

SESAME STIR-FRY

2 tablespoons	**olive or sesame oil**
1 bag (16 ounces)	**frozen vegetable stir-fry mix**
13	**frozen, fully cooked meatballs,** thawed
1/2 cup	**beef broth**
2 tablespoons	**soy sauce**
2 teaspoons	**seasoned rice vinegar**
1/3 cup	**drained canned pineapple chunks**
2 tablespoons	**sesame seeds**
6 cups	**cooked long-grain rice**

In a stir-fry pan or wok, heat oil over medium-high. Toss in vegetables and fry for 5 minutes, stirring frequently. Add meatballs, broth, soy sauce, and vinegar. Stir-fry for 6–7 minutes, or until vegetables are tender. Add the pineapple and stir-fry 3–4 minutes more. Sprinkle sesame seeds over top and serve immediately over hot cooked rice. Makes 4 servings.

SWISS MUSHROOM MEATBALL CASSEROLE

26 (1 pound)	**frozen, fully cooked meatballs,** thawed
1 can (10.5 ounces)	**cream of mushroom soup,** condensed
¾ cup	**milk**
1 can (4 ounces)	**sliced mushrooms,** drained
2 teaspoons	**minced garlic**
1 ½ cups	**grated Swiss cheese**
3 cups	**cooked long-grain white rice**
¼ cup	**grated Parmesan cheese**

Preheat oven to 350 degrees.

In a 9 x 13-inch pan prepared with nonstick cooking spray, combine meatballs, soup, milk, mushrooms, garlic, Swiss cheese, and rice. Sprinkle Parmesan evenly over top and bake 25–30 minutes until bubbly. Makes 6–8 servings.

NOTE: 1 ½ cups water plus ¾ cup rice yields 3 cups hot cooked rice.

CREAMY MEATBALL AND BROWN RICE CASSEROLE

I cup	**uncooked brown rice***
13	**frozen, fully cooked meatballs,** thawed
I cup	**sliced mushrooms**
I can (10.5 ounces)	**cream of mushroom soup,** condensed
I cup	**sour cream**
1/2 teaspoon	**ground black pepper**
1/3 cup	**grated Parmesan cheese**
I 1/2 cups	**crushed Ritz crackers**

Cook brown rice according to package directions. Preheat oven to 350 degrees.

In a large bowl, combine the cooked rice, meatballs, mushrooms, soup, sour cream, and pepper. Spoon mixture into a 9 x 9-inch or 2-quart dish prepared with nonstick cooking spray. Sprinkle Parmesan over top and then cover with crushed crackers. Bake 35–40 minutes, or until bubbly. Makes 5–6 servings.

*I cup uncooked brown rice equals 3 3/4 cups cooked brown rice.

PINEAPPLE MEATBALLS AND RICE

¹/₂ cup	**brown sugar**
1 ¹/₂ tablespoons	**cornstarch**
1 can (20 ounces)	**pineapple chunks,** with juice drained and reserved
¹/₃ cup	**rice vinegar**
1 tablespoon	**soy sauce**
1	**green bell pepper,** seeded and chopped
13	**frozen, fully cooked meatballs,** thawed
4 cups	**hot cooked rice**

In a 2-quart saucepan, combine the brown sugar and cornstarch. Stir in reserved pineapple juice, vinegar, and soy sauce and bring to a boil, stirring every 2 minutes. Add bell pepper and meatballs to the sauce and return to a boil. Reduce heat to medium-high and then cover and simmer 5 minutes. Stir and reduce heat to medium. Stir in pineapple chunks. Simmer 5 minutes more and then serve over the rice. Makes 2–3 servings.

MEATBALLS WITH ORANGE PEANUT SAUCE

3/4 cup	**orange marmalade**
1/4 cup	**peanut butter**
3 tablespoons	**soy sauce**
3 tablespoons	**water**
2 tablespoons	**lemon juice**
1 teaspoon	**minced garlic**
26 (1 pound)	**frozen, fully cooked meatballs,** thawed
6 to 8 cups	**hot cooked rice**

Combine all ingredients except meatballs and rice in a 2- to 3-quart saucepan and bring to a boil, stirring frequently. Fold in the meatballs and return to a boil. Reduce heat to medium and simmer for 8 minutes, or until meatballs are heated through. Serve over the rice. Makes 5–6 servings.

CAJUN SHRIMP AND MEATBALL GOULASH

2 cans (14.5 ounces each)	**diced tomatoes with herb seasoning,** with liquid
1/3 cup	**chopped onion**
1 teaspoon	**Cajun seasoning***
26 (1 pound)	**frozen, fully cooked meatballs**
1 can (14 ounces)	**chicken broth**
1 teaspoon	**minced garlic**
1 1/4 cups	**uncooked long-grain white rice**
1/2 pound	**frozen, fully cooked, peeled, and deveined medium shrimp,** thawed

In a 4-quart stockpot, combine the tomatoes, onion, seasoning, meatballs, broth, and garlic and bring to a boil. Stir in the rice and return to a boil. Reduce heat to medium-low and cover. Simmer for 25 minutes, or until rice is tender. Remove tails from shrimp. Stir in shrimp and cook 3–4 minutes. Serve immediately. Makes 8 servings.

*To make Cajun seasoning, combine 1/2 teaspoon chili powder and 1/2 teaspoon paprika.

CREAMY FRENCH ONION MEATBALLS

78 (3 pounds)	**frozen, fully cooked meatballs**
I can (10.5 ounces)	**French onion soup,** condensed
I can (10.5 ounces)	**cream of celery soup,** condensed
½ teaspoon	**ground black pepper**
I cup	**sour cream**
16 cups	**hot cooked rice**

Place the meatballs in a 4- to 6-quart slow cooker prepared with non-stick cooking spray.

In a bowl, stir together the soups and pepper. Spoon mixture evenly over meatballs. Cover and cook on low heat for 4–5 hours. Stir in sour cream. Cover and cook 20–30 minutes more. Serve over the rice. Makes 12–16 servings.

VARIATION: Thaw meatballs. In a 4- to 6-quart stockpot, combine soups and pepper over medium-high heat on the stovetop, stirring occasionally until bubbly. Stir in meatballs. Cover and cook over medium heat for 15 minutes until meatballs are heated through. Stir in sour cream. Continue to cook 5 minutes more. Serve over the rice.

MEATBALLS WITH APRICOT HOISIN SAUCE

1 jar (18 ounces)	**apricot preserves**
1 package (6 ounces)	**dried apricots,** diced
$1/2$ cup	**hoisin sauce**
$1/2$ cup	**rice vinegar**
$1/8$ teaspoon	**crushed red pepper**
1	**red bell pepper,** diced
1	**green bell pepper,** diced
52 (2 pounds)	**frozen, fully cooked meatballs,** thawed
10 cups	**hot cooked rice**

In a 4-quart saucepan, combine the preserves, apricots, hoisin sauce, vinegar, crushed red pepper, and bell peppers. Bring to a boil, stirring occasionally. Stir in meatballs and return to a boil. Reduce heat to medium. Cover and cook for 15 minutes, stirring occasionally. Serve over hot cooked rice. Makes 8–10 servings.

ENCHILADA MEATBALLS

52 (2 pounds)	**frozen, fully cooked meatballs,** thawed
1 jar (16 ounces)	**chunky salsa**
1 can (16 ounces)	**red enchilada sauce**
10 cups	**hot cooked rice**
	grated Monterey Jack cheese

Place meatballs in a 3- to 4^1/$_2$-quart slow cooker prepared with nonstick cooking spray. Pour salsa and enchilada sauce over meatballs. Cover and cook on high heat for 2–3 hours or on low heat for 4–6 hours. Serve over the rice with cheese sprinkled over top. Makes 8–10 servings.

VARIATION: Thaw meatballs. In a 3- to 5-quart pot, combine meatballs, salsa, and enchilada sauce. Bring to a boil on the stovetop. Cover and cook over medium heat for 15–20 minutes, stirring occasionally, until meatballs are heated through. Serve over the rice and sprinkle with cheese.

CREAMY RICE AND MEATBALLS

30	**frozen, fully cooked meatballs,** thawed
I can (10.5 ounces)	**cream of mushroom soup,** condensed
$^1/_2$ cup	**grape jelly**
6 to 8 cups	**hot cooked rice**

Preheat oven to 350 degrees. Place meatballs in an 8 x 8-inch pan.

In a bowl, combine soup and jelly. Pour mixture evenly over meatballs. Bake, uncovered, for 35 minutes, or until meatballs are heated through. Serve over the rice. Makes 6 servings.

VARIATION: This recipe can also be served as an appetizer with toothpicks, minus the rice.

TASTE OF THE ISLANDS MEATBALLS

26 (1 pound)	**frozen, fully cooked meatballs**
1 cup	**chopped onion**
2	**green or red bell peppers,** sliced
1 cup	**beef broth**
1 can (20 ounces)	**pineapple chunks,** with liquid
1 tablespoon	**lemon juice**
1 tablespoon	**soy sauce**
1 tablespoon	**water**
2 tablespoons	**cornstarch**
1 can (11 ounces)	**mandarin oranges,** drained
6 to 8 cups	**hot cooked rice**

Place meatballs in a 3 1/2- to 4-quart slow cooker prepared with nonstick cooking spray. Sprinkle onion and bell peppers over top. Pour broth and pineapple chunks with liquid over vegetable layer. Do not stir. Cover and cook on low heat for 6–7 hours or on high heat for 3 hours.

In a bowl, thoroughly mix the lemon juice, soy sauce, water, and cornstarch until smooth. Stir lemon juice mixture and mandarin oranges into cooked meatballs. Cover and cook on high heat for 20 minutes, or until sauce thickens. Serve over the rice. Makes 6–8 servings.

FAMILY
FAVORITES

MEATBALLS IN
TOMATO AND CORN SAUCE

I can (15.25 ounces)	**whole kernel corn,** with liquid
I can (14.75 ounces)	**cream-style corn**
3	**tomatoes,** seeded and diced
$\frac{1}{2}$ teaspoon	**crushed red pepper**
I tablespoon	**chopped dried cilantro**
$\frac{1}{4}$ cup	**crumbled cooked bacon**
30	**frozen, fully cooked meatballs,** thawed

Add all ingredients except meatballs in the order listed above to
a 4-quart saucepan. Bring mixture to a boil and then stir in meatballs.
Simmer over medium heat for 10 minutes, or until meatballs are heated
through. Makes 6–8 servings.

SWEET AND SOUR MEATBALL KABOBS

I can (8 ounces)	**pineapple chunks,** with juice
I tablespoon	**cornstarch**
1/2 cup	**maple syrup**
1/4 cup	**vinegar**
2 tablespoons	**soy sauce**
2 tablespoons	**ketchup**
1/2 teaspoon	**minced garlic**
I	**medium red or green bell pepper**
I	**red onion,** peeled
18	**frozen, fully cooked meatballs,** thawed
12	**medium whole mushrooms,** with stems

Preheat oven to 350 degrees.

Drain pineapple juice into a saucepan; whisk in cornstarch until smooth. Stir in syrup, vinegar, soy sauce, ketchup, and garlic and bring to a boil. Reduce heat and allow to softly boil for 2 minutes; remove from heat. Cut bell pepper in half and clean out. Cut each half into 6 equal pieces. Cut onion into 12 equal pieces. On 6 metal skewers, place a meatball, a mushroom, onion, bell pepper, and pineapple chunk. Repeat one more time, ending with the meatball. Place skewers on a large baking sheet and brush with half of the prepared sauce. Bake for 10 minutes; turn and brush with remaining sauce. Bake 10–15 minutes more, or until done. Serve immediately. Makes 6 servings.

VARIATION: Place kabobs on a hot grill. Baste with sauce. Every 2–3 minutes give kabobs a quarter turn, basting with more sauce. Grill until done.

NOTE: If using bamboo skewers, soak in water for 30 minutes prior to assembling kabobs.

CAESAR MEATBALL KABOBS

18	**frozen, fully cooked meatballs,** thawed
1	**medium yellow or green bell pepper,** seeded and cut into 12 equal pieces
1	**large or 2 small yellow summer squash,** cut into 12 (1 1/2- to 2-inch) slices
12	**whole mushrooms**
12	**cherry tomatoes**
1/2 cup	**Caesar dressing**
1/4 teaspoon	**ground black pepper**

On a long metal skewer, thread a meatball, bell pepper slice, yellow squash slice, mushroom, and tomato. Repeat pattern ending with a meatball. Repeat for 5 more skewers. Combine Caesar dressing and black pepper. Place meatball skewers directly on a hot grill. Baste the kabobs with the dressing. Grill for 6–8 minutes, turning and basting every 2–3 minutes until done. Makes 6 kabobs.

NOTE: If using bamboo skewers, soak in water for 30 minutes prior to assembling kabobs.

BREAKFAST BURRITOS

¹/₂ cup	**chopped onion**
¹/₂ cup	**chopped green or red bell pepper**
I teaspoon	**olive oil**
7	**frozen, fully cooked meatballs,** thawed and finely chopped
4	**eggs**
¹/₄ teaspoon	**ground black pepper**
4 (6-inch)	**flour tortillas**
4 tablespoons	**grated cheddar cheese,** divided
4 tablespoons	**fresh salsa,** divided

In a frying pan over medium-high heat, saute the onion and bell pepper in oil until tender. Add meatballs pieces to vegetables and saute 2 minutes. Scramble eggs and black pepper into vegetable and meat mixture. Continue to stir until egg mixture is completely cooked. Divide egg mixture over individual warm tortillas. Sprinkle I tablespoon each of cheese and salsa over mixture. Fold to form a burrito. Makes 4 servings.

EASY MEATBALL PIZZA

1 (12-inch)	**pre-made pizza crust**
1 jar (14 ounces)	**pizza sauce,** divided
1 1/2 cups	**grated mozzarella or cheddar cheese,** divided
13	**frozen, fully cooked meatballs**
1/4 teaspoon	**Italian seasoning**

Preheat oven to 400 degrees.

Place pizza crust on a pizza pan. Spread 1 cup pizza sauce over crust. Sprinkle half the cheese over sauce. Place meatballs and 2 teaspoons water in a microwave-safe bowl and microwave on high for 3 minutes; drain any excess liquid. Cut each meatball in half and then toss with the remaining sauce. Spoon meatballs over cheese layer assuring the cut side is down. Layer remaining cheese over meatballs. Sprinkle Italian seasoning evenly over pizza. Bake for 12–15 minutes, or until cheese is melted and sauce is bubbly. Cut pizza into 8 slices. Makes 4–6 servings.

SOUTHWEST CRESCENT POCKETS

18	**frozen, fully cooked meatballs,** thawed
2 tubes (8 ounces each)	**refrigerated crescent rolls**
I can (4 ounces)	**diced green chiles,** drained
8 tablespoons	**grated cheddar or Mexican-blend cheese,** divided
4 tablespoons	**finely chopped onion,** divided
	salsa and sour cream, optional

Preheat oven to 375 degrees.

Crumble meatballs into a large frying pan and saute 6–8 minutes until browned. Roll crescent dough from I tube onto a baking sheet. Separate dough into 4 rectangles, pressing the triangle edges together to form rectangles. Spoon chiles evenly over each rectangle leaving $^1/_2$-inch around the edge. Divide crumbled cooked meatballs evenly over chiles. Sprinkle I tablespoon cheese and I tablespoon onion over meat. Unroll remaining crescent roll dough and separate dough into 4 rectangles. Place rectangles over the top of each filled rectangle. Press dough around the edges to seal. Sprinkle I tablespoon cheese over each crescent pocket. Bake I3 minutes, or until golden brown. Garnish with salsa and sour cream if desired. Makes 4 servings.

MEATBALL POT PIE

2 cups	**frozen mixed vegetables,** thawed and drained
13 frozen	**frozen, fully cooked meatballs,** thawed
2 cans (10.5 ounces each)	**cream of mushroom soup,** condensed
1 can (15 ounces)	**diced potatoes,** drained
1 teaspoon	**chopped dried rosemary**
1/3 cup	**milk**
2	**frozen or refrigerated piecrusts,** at room temperature

Preheat oven to 400 degrees.

In a 2-quart bowl, combine all the ingredients except the crusts. Place one piecrust evenly over the bottom and sides of a deep-dish pie pan, pressing it up the sides. Fill the piecrust with the meatball mixture. Cover with the second crust, sealing the edges and cutting slits in the top to vent steam. Bake 45 minutes, or until golden brown. Allow to cool 5 minutes before serving. Makes 6 servings.

INSTANT SOFT TACO

5	**frozen, fully cooked meatballs**
1	**flour tortilla**
1 tablespoon	**grated Monterey Jack cheese**
2 tablespoons	**salsa**
1 tablespoon	**guacamole**
1/2 tablespoon	**sour cream**
	chopped fresh cilantro, optional

Cook meatballs according to package directions in the microwave. Serve hot meatballs in a warm flour tortilla with cheese, salsa, guacamole, and sour cream. Garnish with cilantro if desired. Makes 1 serving.

NOTE: This recipe can be doubled, tripled, or quadrupled depending on the number of tacos needed.

MEATBALL FAJITA QUESADILLAS

I	**small onion,** sliced
I	**red bell pepper,** sliced
I tablespoon	**olive oil**
$^1/_2$ teaspoon	**garlic salt**
20	**frozen, fully cooked meatballs**
4 (10-inch)	**burrito-size flour tortillas**
I cup	**grated Colby Jack cheese**
	salsa and guacamole, optional

In a frying pan, saute the onion and bell pepper in oil until tender. Sprinkle garlic salt over top. While vegetables are sauteing, place meatballs in a microwave-safe dish. Drizzle I tablespoon water over top and microwave on high for 3 minutes, stirring once in the middle of cooking time. Cut each heated meatball into three slices.

Prepare a large frying pan with nonstick cooking spray. On half of each tortilla, layer 2 tablespoons cheese, 15 meatball slices, one-fourth of the sauteed vegetable mixture, and 2 tablespoons cheese. Fold the empty half of the tortilla over the layered half. Place the quesadilla in the heated pan and cook 2–3 minutes on each side, or until golden crisp. Repeat for the remaining quesadillas. Cooked quesadillas can be placed in a pan and put in a preheated 180-degree oven to keep warm until ready to be served. Cut each quesadilla in half and serve with salsa and guacamole. Makes 4 servings.

BAKED BEEFY
MAC AND CHEESE

26 (I pound)	**frozen, fully cooked meatballs**
2 boxes (7.25 ounces each)	**macaroni and cheese dinner**
2 cans (10.5 ounces each)	**cream of mushroom soup,** condensed
1 1/2 cups	**milk**
2	**medium tomatoes,** thinly sliced
3 tablespoons	**grated Parmesan cheese**

Preheat oven to 350 degrees.

Cook frozen meatballs on a baking sheet for 20 minutes. While meatballs bake, cook macaroni dinner according to package directions. Drain the water from the pan. Stir soup, milk, and cheese packets into the cooked macaroni. Place meatballs in a 9 x 13-inch pan prepared with nonstick cooking spray. Spoon mixture evenly over the meatball layer. Lay tomato slices over top and then sprinkle the Parmesan cheese over top. Bake, uncovered, for 25–30 minutes. Makes 6–8 servings.

STUFFING-COVERED MEATBALL CASSEROLE

1 box (6 ounces)	**stuffing mix,** any variety
1 can (10.5 ounces)	**cream of mushroom soup,** condensed
¼ cup	**milk**
2 cups	**frozen mixed vegetables**
26 (1 pound)	**frozen, fully cooked meatballs,** thawed
1 cup	**grated Colby Jack cheese**

Preheat oven to 400 degrees.

Prepare stuffing according to package directions. In a 9 x 13-inch pan prepared with nonstick cooking spray, combine the soup and milk. Stir in the vegetables. Evenly place meatballs over the vegetable mixture. Sprinkle cheese over top. Spoon prepared stuffing evenly over casserole. Bake, uncovered, for 25–30 minutes. Makes 6–8 servings.

ENCHILADA CASSEROLE

39 (1 ½ pounds)	**frozen, fully cooked meatballs,** thawed
1	**medium red onion,** finely chopped
1 ½ teaspoons	**ground cumin**
1 can (28 ounces)	**enchilada sauce**
18	**corn tortillas**
1 cup	**grated Colby Jack cheese**

Preheat oven to 350 degrees.

Crumble meatballs into a large frying pan. Stir in onion and cumin. Saute for 6–8 minutes, or until onion is tender. Place enchilada sauce in a round container deep enough to hold it, and wide enough to dip the tortillas. Dip both sides of each tortilla liberally in the enchilada sauce. Cover the bottom of a 9 x 13-inch pan prepared with nonstick cooking spray with 6 dipped tortillas. (Tortillas will overlap a little.) Sprinkle half the meatball mixture and one-third of the cheese over the tortillas. Cover with 6 more tortillas dipped in sauce. Sprinkle remaining meatball mixture and one-third of the cheese over tortilla layer. Cover with the remaining tortillas dipped in sauce. Pour remaining sauce evenly over tortillas and sprinkle remaining cheese on top. Bake for 25 minutes. Makes 8–10 servings.

SPICY MEATBALL BURRITOS

1	**medium onion,** chopped
1 tablespoon	**olive oil**
13	**frozen, fully cooked meatballs,** thawed and halved
1 can (7 ounces)	**diced green chiles**
1 envelope	**taco seasoning**
6 (8-inch)	**flour tortillas,** warmed
1 can (15 ounces)	**black beans,** rinsed and drained
1 1/2 cups	**grated Monterey Jack or Mexican-blend cheese**
1 can (16 ounces)	**green enchilada sauce,** divided

In a large frying pan, saute the onion in the oil until tender over medium-high heat. Stir meatball halves and chiles into the onion. Sprinkle taco seasoning evenly over top and stir. Cook for 5 minutes, or until mixture is hot. On individual tortillas, layer black beans, meatball mixture, cheese, and 1 tablespoon enchilada sauce. Fold ends over filling and wrap burrito style. Top with a dollop of sour cream and serve over a bed of shredded lettuce if desired. Makes 6 servings.

TATER TOT KID'S CASSEROLE

26 (1 pound)	**frozen, fully cooked meatballs,** thawed and quartered
1 can (14.5 ounces)	**cut green beans,** drained
1 can (10.5 ounces)	**cream of mushroom soup,** condensed
1 bag (27–32 ounces)	**frozen tater tots**

Arrange meatball pieces in a 9 x 13-inch pan prepared with nonstick cooking spray. Evenly place green beans over meatball layer and then spread soup over top. Cover with tater tots, laying them on their sides. Bake 40–50 minutes. Makes 6–8 servings.

VARIATION: Saute 1 chopped onion in 1 tablespoon olive oil. Layer over meatball layer and continue with the recipe as directed.

HASH BROWN MEATBALL CASSEROLE

1 bag (28 ounces)	**frozen cubed hash brown potatoes with onions and peppers**
1 cup	**sour cream**
1 can (10.5 ounces)	**cream of mushroom soup,** condensed
1 1/2 cups	**grated Colby Jack or cheddar cheese**
24	**frozen, fully cooked meatballs**

Preheat oven to 350 degrees.

In a large bowl, combine the hash browns, sour cream, soup, and cheese. Spread potato mixture in a 9 x 13-inch pan prepared with nonstick cooking spray. Evenly place meatballs over the top. Cover pan with aluminum foil and bake 45 minutes. Uncover and bake 20–25 minutes more, or until bubbly. Makes 6–8 servings.

KID-FRIENDLY TACO CASSEROLE

26 (1 pound)	**frozen, fully cooked meatballs,** thawed
2 cans (8 ounces each)	**tomato sauce**
1 envelope	**taco seasoning mix**
10	**medium flour tortillas**
1 can (10.5 ounces)	**cream of chicken soup,** condensed
$3/4$ cup	**milk**
1 $1/2$ cups	**grated cheddar or Mexican-blend cheese**

Preheat oven to 350 degrees.

Crumble the meatballs into a large frying pan and saute over medium heat for 6 minutes, or until browned. Stir in tomato sauce and taco seasoning. Reduce heat to medium-low and simmer 5 minutes. Use 6 tortillas to cover bottom and sides of a 9 x 13-inch pan prepared with nonstick cooking spray. Spread meatball mixture over tortillas. Use remaining tortillas to cover, cutting to fit if necessary.

In a bowl, combine the soup and milk, and then pour over tortillas. Sprinkle cheese over top. Bake 20–25 minutes, or until edges turn golden brown. Makes 6–8 servings.

VARIATION: Saute crumbled meatballs with 1 cup chopped onion until onion is tender. You can also add 1 can (4 ounces) diced green chiles for a spicier version.

NOTES

NOTES

NOTES

NOTES

NOTES

NOTES

NOTES

Metric Conversion Chart

Liquid and Dry Measures

U.S.	Canadian	Australian
¼ teaspoon	1 mL	1 ml
½ teaspoon	2 mL	2 ml
1 teaspoon	5 mL	5 ml
1 tablespoon	15 mL	20 ml
¼ cup	50 mL	60 ml
⅓ cup	75 mL	80 ml
½ cup	125 mL	125 ml
⅔ cup	150 mL	170 ml
¾ cup	175 mL	190 ml
1 cup	250 mL	250 ml
1 quart	1 liter	1 litre

Temperature Conversion Chart

Fahrenheit	Celsius
250	120
275	140
300	150
325	160
350	180
375	190
400	200
425	220
450	230
475	240
500	260

 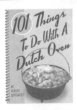   

ABOUT THE AUTHOR

Stephanie Ashcraft, author of the original *101 Things To Do With A Cake Mix*, has taught cooking classes based on the tips and meals in her cookbooks for almost ten years. She lives in Tucson, Arizona, with her husband and four children. Samples from this book have made her a favorite neighbor in her community. Stephanie, a native of Kirklin, Indiana, graduated from Brigham Young University with a degree in family science. This is her 13th cookbook.